BRING OUR
BABY HOME

BRING OUR BABY HOME

MY MEMOIRS OF THE VIETNAM WAR
First Tour, June 1967 thru June 1968

Leon Rodriguez

authorHOUSE®

AuthorHouse™
1663 Liberty Drive
Bloomington, IN 47403
www.authorhouse.com
Phone: 1-800-839-8640

Published by AuthorHouse   08/29/2012

ISBN: 978-1-4772-6321-1 (sc)
ISBN: 978-1-4772-6320-4 (hc)
ISBN: 978-1-4772-6319-8 (e)

Library of Congress Control Number: 2012915568

"Bring Our Baby Home is the true meaning of a Vietnam Soldier in Vietnam, and his wife 13,000 miles away in the U.S. coming together to save the life of a deserted baby. It shows the true meaning of love, affection and a U.S. army Medic saving a life."

Arthur L. Guerrero
Golden, CO

*SGT Guerrero earned the Combat Infantry Badge, was awarded The Silver Star Medal for heroism and The Bronze Star Medal. He also received The Purple Heart Medal for combat injuries.

"Bring Our Baby Home is quite a surprise, extremely informative and quite emotional. The history Sergeant Rodriguez is providing will be a revelation to most and a treasure of the highest caliber for generations to come."

Staff Sergeant Michael Collins, U.S. Army Retired
Aurora, CO

*SSG Collins was a Light Weapons Ranger Infantryman with the 1st Air Cavalry Division. He earned the Combat Infantry Badge, was awarded The Bronze Star Medal and received The Purple Heart Medal for combat injuries.

ACKNOWLEDGEMENTS

I dedicate this true story to the finest collection of Doctors, Nurses & Corpsmen ever assembled in one U.S. Army Medical facility. Their care and treatment of our troops wounded in the Vietnam War was the very best possible.

Special thanks to my wife, Else, and my children, Barbara, Patricia, Lisa and Nick for asking me to put this story on paper. Also, thanks to my friend, Jack Henderson, for his encouragement and direction.

PROLOGUE

B RING OUR BABY HOME is a true accounting of the challenges
I faced as a U.S. Army Sergeant helping my Unit, The U.S. Army
24th Evacuation Hospital, achieve its mission of saving lives of patients
that had been seriously wounded in The Vietnam War during the time
period of June 1967 through June 1968. This story also tells of the
challenges I met in trying to save the life of a newborn Vietnamese
baby girl that had been deserted by her parents and left at the 24th
Evacuation Hospital.

26 SEPTEMBER 1967
@ 2000 HRS.

The Viet Cong (V.C.) are working an area north of Bien Hoa searching the small hamlets around the rice paddies for suspected Republic of South Vietnam and American sympathizers and supporters. The V.C. happened upon a tiny village and began threats and interrogation. The villagers are very poor and their living conditions are more basic than you can imagine. These people do not care who is in charge of Vietnam, all these primitive souls want is to be left alone in peace. Unfortunately for the villagers the Soldiers of The Army of the Republic of Vietnam (ARVN) was right behind the Viet Cong and a firefight quickly erupted.

The V.C. not only fired at the ARVNs, but also upon the defenseless villagers. The ARVNs called in American Army Air Support and the U.S. Soldiers quickly arrived in UH-1 Helicopters (Huey Gunships) to support the ARVNs. The battle lasted only a few minutes as most of the V.C. were killed or ran away. There were no injuries to the U.S. Soldiers or the ARVNs, but several of the villagers were killed or wounded. One of the injured was a very pregnant woman who had sustained a gunshot to the abdomen. The U.S. medics administered immediate care and loaded the woman, her husband and young son onto the helicopter for transport to the 24th Evacuation Hospital for treatment. At the 24th Evacuation Hospital Emergency Room the injured lady was given more pain medication and another I.V. was started. She was moved quickly through x-ray & lab and had the usual pre-op care. She was taken into the Pre-op ward where she had to wait for the availability of an open operating room table and surgical crew. The 24th Evacuation Hospital is a very busy treatment facility and the policy is to treat all Americans before anyone else. The wounded lady got into surgery after 2200 hrs. (10 P.M). The 24th Evacuation Hospital had most surgical specialties, but did not have an OB/GYN specialist. The available General Surgeon assessed that before he could repair her bowels she must have a Caesarean section in able to have room to work. The C-section was quick and produced twin baby girls. The two babies are non-reactive to stimulus, are not breathing, are cold and blue. The Surgical Nurse placed the babies on a chux pad on a wheeled stainless steel utility cart to be bagged and sent to the mortuary. The surgeon closed the woman's uterus and began the job of finding the bullet perforations and removing the damaged intestines and doing an anastomosis (reconnecting the bowels) of the guts so that they would once again function in a normal fashion. Meanwhile, a surgical technician, Specialist Bill McGillivary, walked into the operating room area and thought he saw movement of one of the babies. McGilivary stopped and flipped the toe of the baby and it moved, so he flipped the toe of the other baby and it moved.

McGilvary said, "Hey Doc, I believe these babies are alive!"

The Surgeon replied, "Get them to the Recovery Room the nurses know what to do!"

McGillivary wheeled the babies into the Recovery Room and the Nurses began cleaning off the blood and Vernix Caseosa on the babies. They found two cardboard boxes and cut a white cotton blanket for padding in the boxes and to cover the babies. The Nurses covered the boxes with clear perforated food wrap and inserted an oxygen line into each box and they placed warm irrigation containers in the boxes to help warm the babies. The babies began moving and appeared to be breathing normally. The cardboard boxes were labeled Baby #1 and Baby #2. A little later the Nurses named the babies Sandy and Cindy. The Nurses definitely did not like the babies being labeled with numbers. The Mom was out of surgery at midnight and all settled in for a nights rest with the lady's husband and son sleeping under her bed and the two new babies at each side in their cardboard boxes.

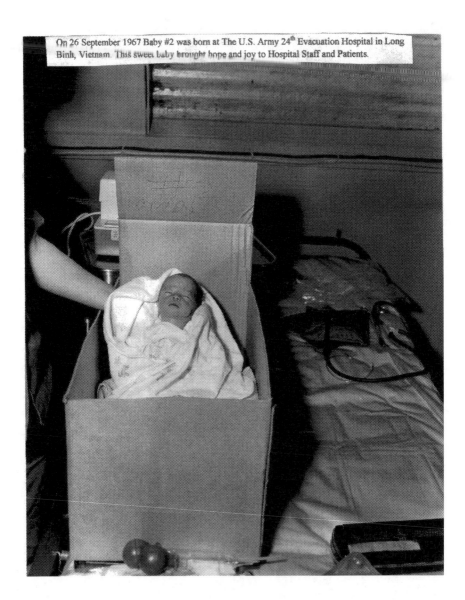

On 26 September 1967 Baby #2 was born at The U.S. Army 24th Evacuation Hospital in Long Binh, Vietnam. This sweet baby brought hope and joy to Hospital Staff and Patients.

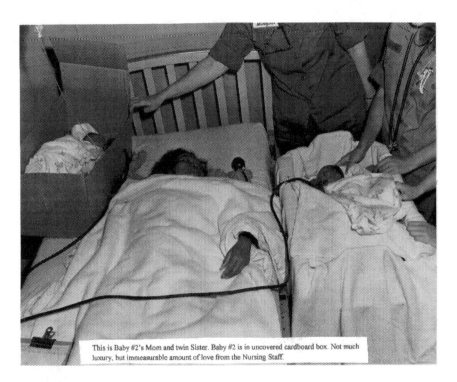

This is Baby #2's Mom and twin Sister. Baby #2 is in uncovered cardboard box. Not much luxury, but immeasurable amount of love from the Nursing Staff.

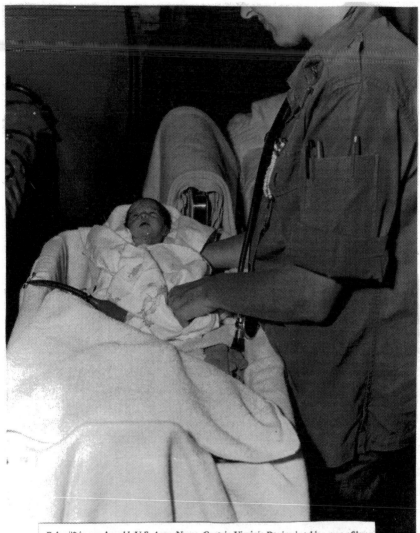

Baby #2 is one day old. U.S. Army Nurse, Captain Virginia Devine is taking care of her.

27 SEPTEMBER
@ 0600

I left the Senior NCO (non-commissioned officer) tent (the hootch where I slept) and walked through the lightly falling rain over to the complex of Quonset huts which is the 24th Evacuation Hospital. I walked into the central surgical Quonset hut and my night shift NCO in charge, Sergeant Trimble, warmly greeted me and said there is no major breakdown of equipment and everything is going smoothly.

Sergeant Trimble has a large smile as he said, "Sergeant Rod, we had a little productive surgery last night! We delivered twin baby girls!"

I said, "That is a good thing!"

I went about my duties and later found myself just as curious as the rest of the Operating Room Staff in needing to see the newborn babies. I went into the Quonset hut that housed the I.C.U/Pre-op/Post-op Recovery area. Captain Virginia Devine is the Nurse in charge. You may have heard the expression, "Good looking gals are good," yes, Virginia Devine is a very beautiful woman and also a professional highly competent U.S. Army Nurse.

Captain Devine smiled and said, "So even the hard core NCO is curious?"

I said, "Captain Devine, may I have a look see?"

She said, "Of course, maybe someday you will be a daddy."

I passed the many beds filled with injured Soldiers, Marines, ARVNs, Civilians, even some V.C. Then I saw the Vietnamese mom, her baby girls on each side in cardboard boxes and her husband and young son under her bed. The mom got my complete attention; her eyes were sooo big and wide open. I didn't know if it was pain, fear, astonishment, wonder or just 'what the hell is going on.' This woman who had never been inside a real building, never known electricity, air-conditioning, beds, sheets, pillows, or had never had medical attention with all of the gadgets. Then I looked at the babies. My Goodness, they are so very small as they lay covered with their white cotton blankets in cardboard boxes labeled #1 Sandy and #2 Cindy. My mind is a little clouded as I think of these two precious babies and how innocent they are and all caught up in this ugly war. I looked at the Dad, I don't believe he ever visited a barber, he had small clumps of long facial hair, his teeth (what few he had) were dark brown and broken. He looked to be less than five feet tall, but his feet are huge. I'm sure he has never worn shoes in his life; the soles of his feet are calloused at least ½ an inch. His hands are scarred and work worn. He wore only a dirty white thong and a tee shirt one of the corpsmen had given him. The little boy was said to be six years old, but looked more like a small four year old. He wore filthy red shorts.

Later that evening, I thought about what Captain Devine had said, 'Maybe someday you will be a daddy."

In Vietnam, most of us communicated with our wives or loved ones with the miniature audio cassettes. I got a cassette off tonight to my wife telling her about the unusual occurrence of the birth of twin baby girls in our surgery. My wife, Else, and I have been married for over four years. No baby. We really wanted a child. My wife had seen the doctor to make sure we could have kids. The doctor said just relax, the kids will come. Else went as far as taking prescribed pills to prevent pregnancy as it was believed that when stopping the pill she would be more fertile and susceptible to pregnancy.

"Oh well, what kind of dad would a career soldier be."

28 SEPTEMBER 1967

I began my usual routine and met with Sergeant Trimble. His face had the expression of sadness.

I said, "Sergeant Trimble, what is the problem?"

Sergeant Trimble replied, "Baby #1, Sandy, has died."

The entire O.R. Staff, Pre-op, Post-op folks are all deeply saddened with the loss of this innocent baby.

2 OCTOBER 1967

The Vietnamese mom had recovered quite nicely and was scheduled to be discharged from our hospital. Arrangements had been made for the family to go to a tent city just outside of Saigon that held refugees and displaced persons. That is when the shit hit the fan. The mom refused to take Baby #2.

The mom got very emotional, the translator told our hospital Staff and Administrators that the mom said, "If one baby dies, then the other baby should die also."

The mom screamed, cried and carried on until the Vietnamese authorities asked if the baby could stay for a while until arrangements could be made with an orphanage. The translator explained that these are Montagnard people and they are a very superstitious tribe. The 24th Evacuation Hospital Administrator reluctantly agreed. Before the mom left she named the baby Nguyen Thi Mein.

Captain Devine and her Staff are elated that Baby #2 will stay with them. Captain Devine knows full well that Baby #2 would die if she left our hospital. A very premature baby needs careful care, oxygen, cleanliness, proper nourishment, nursing and love.

9 OCTOBER 1967

G ood news. Today Hanoi announced that it would observe a seven day truce from 27 January to 3 February 1968 in honor of the TET Holiday. Such truces had been honored in the past—The North Vietnamese usually used the truce period (which meant a short halt in U.S. bombing as well) to re-supply, and the South Vietnamese used truces to allow many of its troops to take a short leave.

Baby #2 is doing well. Care packages arrive frequently with baby clothes, baby powder, baby shampoo, diapers and similac. The Hospital Carpenters have made a crib for Baby #2. Baby #2 is a celebrity patient, in fact all the 24th Evacuation Hospital Staff loves this tiny infant.

I must give you a visual of what Baby #2's home looks like. The Quonset huts are long rectangular buildings. As you walk into the main entrance on the right are a dozen beds that are for the I.C.U. Patients, as you continue along to the right is a plywood tunnel that leads into x-ray & lab. Across the tunnel to the right are a dozen beds for the Pre-op Patients. At the end of the hut is a door that leads outside where the litters are kept for carrying off the dead to the mortuary after the bodies have been bagged and tagged. Walking back to the front of the hut are where the, all too frequently, inoperable comatose dying Patients lay, (usually most of their heads are blown off) they are in fact dead but their young hearts continue to beat. Continuing on is another plywood tunnel that leads into the Operating Room Area. Then moving on is the Nursing Station with Baby #2 nearby in a crudely constructed crib. Continuing toward the front door are a dozen more beds for the Post-op Recovery Patients.

There are no words that can adequately thank and compliment the I.C.U./Pre-op/Post-op Recovery Staff of the 24th Evacuation Hospital for their outstanding care given to our injured servicemen during their critical time of need.

11 November 1967

More of the same old, same old. The war is getting worse and the causality count is greater every day. The only bright light is that Baby #2 is growing like a weed and is so full of smiles. With the number of injured greatly increasing the Operating Room Staff are working their butts off and not complaining. There is a little grumbling from a couple of surgeons, but that does not affect their job performance. The surgeons put in more hours of duty than one can imagine.

I must mention that the weather has changed from the rainy monsoon season to the very hot dry season. The red dust is everywhere.

Dear reader, I feel that I must share with you a little more of Baby #2's home.

Our unit's designation is:

> The U.S. Army 24th Evacuation Hospital, located in Long Binh, South Vietnam.

Our Patients are comprised of:

> U.S. Army
> U.S. Marines
> U.S. Air Force

U.S. Navy

Army of the Republic of Vietnam

Republic of Korea (ROK) Tiger Division

Royal Thai Army

Australian Servicemen

Vietnamese Civilians

Cambodians

Laotians

North Vietnam Army

Viet Cong (V.C.)

American Civilians: U.S. Government Employees, Air
   America, Red Cross workers

Other Foreign Civilians

U.S. Contract Workers: Vinell Power, PA&E,
   RMKBRJ

The following is the list of surgical specialties of the 24th Evacuation
Hospital:

Neuro Surgery

Thoracic Surgery

Vascular Surgery

Orthopedic Surgery

Genitourinary Surgery

Maxillofacial Surgery

Plastic Surgery

General Surgery

The Neuro Surgeons do mostly craniotomies for injuries caused by
high velocity trauma (Claymore mines, bullets and shrapnel) and low

velocity trauma (bulky objects to the head, spent rounds, blunt trauma to the head). This is a sad case study of kinetic energy. The Orthopedic Surgeons keep busy with an incredible array of fractured bone injuries caused by about anything you can imagine. The Vascular Surgeons keep busy trying to save hands, feet, arms and legs by doing vascular reconstruction. The General Surgeons are busy with abdominal trauma, soft tissue wounds, delayed primary closures, tumors, appendectomies, goring's (water buffalos) and multiple fragment wounds. The Eye Surgeons do enucleations (removal of eye), cataracts and removal of foreign bodies in the eye. Plastic Surgeons do plastic repairs of the face and revisions of scars and cleft palate reconstructions. The Genitourinary Surgeons do nephrectomies (removal of kidney), repair ureters and bladder injuries. The Maxillofacial Surgeons are part of the WRAIR team (Walter Reed Army Institute of Research). This group has the latest in facial reconstruction and repair tools. In fact they have a complete ASIF kit made by the Swiss. This kit contains mini templates, screws, plates, taps, drills, and bending rods designed for facial injuries. The 24th Evacuation Hospital with specialists from Walter Reed Research Team is the first American hospital to use these tools.

Our Operating Rooms actually ran a schedule. For the most part there are few battle causalities in the morning (except for head injuries which there are so many that the Neuro Surgeons operate almost 24/7 as the 24th Evacuation Hospital is the Neuro Surgery Center). The schedule is made up of; delayed primary closures (wounds that cannot be closed at the initial time of surgery usually because of high risk of infection), cases referred from MEDCAP (Medical Civil Action Program) such as cleft palate reconstruction, cataracts, tumors and scar revisions.

Late in the afternoon, evening and late night we receive most battle casualties. Early morning and mid-morning we could usually catch up with the back-log.

20 NOVEMBER 1967

This is the beginning of difficult times for me in maintaining special supply needs for surgery. Many items required for surgery are not in the U.S. Army Medical Supply Catalog. Examples:

Fogarty embolectomy catheters, which are used to draw out old blood clots that are lodged in the injured arteries, a real must to save a limb (the blood clots are caused from prolonged use of tourniquet).

Vascular forceps, vascular scissors, vessel loops, which are used for arterial and venous reconstruction.

Malleable suction/cautery tips, which is the main tool used by Neuro Surgeons to clear a surgical field and cauterize small vessels.

The list goes on and the 24th Evacuation Hospital Supply Officer tells me, "If the Army wanted you to have these items they would be in the Medical Supply Catalog."

As an NCO in charge of Operating Rooms since 1959 I am an expert on ordering standard or non-standard medical supplies. I know what I am talking about. My job is not to argue with this clown and the Surgeons cannot operate with my excuses. So, I write to NCO's around the world in U.S. Army Hospitals and ask for their help. I received supplies from The 106th General Hospital in Japan, from Letterman Army Hospital, from Fitzsimons Army Hospital and Walter Reed Army Hospital. Also, I contacted my friends in country, the 93rd Evacuation Hospital, the 3rd Field Hospital, the 12th Evacuation Hospital. We got many of the special items we need to care for our Patients. I remember a note attached from a package from SFC David Bustos saying "Nothing but the best for troops in Vietnam." SFC Herb Null the 12th Evacuation Hospital in Cu Chi, Vietnam sent needed supplies. Herb Null was my best man when I got married on 25 October 1963 in Ludwigsburg, Germany.

26 NOVEMBER 1967

O ur MEDCAP Program focus is in and around the Bien Hoa Province. We set up a tent and exam tables. The locals are lined up and waiting for us to check out their medical problems. We go with several Doctors, Nurses and Corpsmen. We see toddlers that are totally emaciated, but have huge bloated stomachs filled with worms, we have many children with cleft palates, we have many Patients with cataracts from the age of eighteen months to eighty-five years old. After the cataract patients have their surgery our Optometrist fits them with two pair of glasses provided by The Lions Clubs of America. We schedule Patients for removal of tumors and scar revisions. For these people we get to care for it is like a miracle.

Baby #2 is blossoming and appears to be happy. I truly feel good visiting this little person as she seems to lift my spirits and she seems safe and comfortable in my arms. I have never heard this baby cry.

1 DECEMBER 1967

This month is starting off good. SFC Herb Null of the 12th Evacuation Hospital in Cu Chi, sent over some much needed items; 4-0 silk suture (which is the Neuro Surgeons choice suture for closing the dura (tissue covering the brain and spinal cord) and the General Surgeons choice suture for bowel anastomosis. He also sent a good supply of silver clips need for ligating tiny arteries and veins in the brain.

3 DECEMBER 1967

I make my first trip to Saigon. I visited the 3rd Field Hospital and meet with the Medical Supply Officer. I cannot remember his name, his rank was Major and he is a MSC Officer (Medical Service Corps) and he told me that his father is a U.S. Army General. This guy is a real gentleman and was great help in giving me many much needed supplies. This trip to Saigon is very productive as a couple of Special Forces Advisors invited me to their compound where they train ARVNs. The Green Berets gave me desperately needed salt tablets and cases of hydrogen peroxide. I had been told prior to leaving Long Binh that the Louis Pasteur Medical School is directly across from the Special Forces compound so I loaded up with obsolete medical journals and medical books to give to the Medical School. The folks at the school are overjoyed at my gifts.

In case you are wondering why I need salt tablets and peroxide I will explain. The salt tablets are for mixing with distilled water in making normal saline, which is used in large quantities for the irrigation of wounds. Hydrogen peroxide is also used in copious amounts for wound irrigation. Many times we use over a gallon of saline or peroxide on one Patient.

6 December 1967

I make a short trip to the small town of Tan Hiep. Again, my Green Beret friends give me access to more medical supplies. This is another Special Forces Training Camp for ARVNs. On this compound they actually have a real swimming pool. Next to the pool is an air-conditioned Quonset hut used as their mess hall, which actually served meals on china with real knives, forks and spoons. "They are living well!!"

10 DECEMBER 1967

Today I am all caught up, surgery is not too busy. I am able to go along with the MEDCAP Volunteers. After helping screen potential Patients for surgery I was invited to go to an orphanage with a couple of Green Beret buddies and a couple of ARVNs. The orphanage is something I am truly not prepared for. It is a small walled in compound with three buildings. Three Nuns run the place. One small building is for storage, another small building is the kitchen and the larger building housed the children. I do not recall the large building having any doors and there are large openings where there should have been windows or at least screens. The stench of this place is overpowering. There are three large open rooms that have toddlers and little babies stacked on shelves (like a library) in boxes that look like dresser drawers. The babies are covered with flies and strange looking bugs, and the babies are lying in their own urine and feces. Many of the babies are missing an eye, an arm, or a foot, or a hand, or a leg. Many of them have open draining and festering wounds. Many of the babies are half Vietnamese and half Caucasian, or half Vietnamese and half Black. These babies have one thing in common, "Nobody wants them." At this moment I wish with all my heart that the people that so favor war could see how the innocent suffer. We left some food that my friends had brought and the Nuns are very grateful.

That evening as I sent off an audio cassette to my wife, I told her of the orphanage. I could hardly hold back the tears while describing the pathetic conditions of the orphanage.

15 December 1967

It is mid-December 1967 and we are running desperately low on medical supplies and my answer from the Medical Supply Officer is "Due Out." I ask to look at the medical supply warehouse shelves.

The Medical Supply Officer said, "Go ahead and look Sergeant. See those little white slips of paper? That's where the items are supposed to be, but the items are due/out just like the disposition forms I send you say, when we don't have the item."

I said, "But Sir, the other hospital facilities and Evacs in Vietnam are receiving their supplies."

The officer responded, "Sergeant Rodriguez, you are bordering on insubordination, when I get supplies you get supplies, you are dismissed."

Trouble comes in bunches. Here in good ole South Vietnam it's getting hotter and hotter, and dustier and dustier. The operating room air-conditioners are acting up and sputtering and mostly not cooling the surgery area adequately. I call the U.S. Army Corps of Engineers. After I explain my situation the answering clerk says, "Sergeant, We will put you on our list and get to you when your turn comes up."

I said, "Hold on man, I need A.C. now, the operating rooms must be at a lower temperature. Our wounded patients already come to us with a fever and we must keep them from getting any hotter."

The clerk said, "Look Sarge, we have twenty-five trailers that house Generals and Bird Colonels and we must service them as our first priorities."

I said, "Bull Shit!! My Patients come first, to hell with a bunch of Generals and Colonels!!"

The clerk says, "Don't get pissed with me Sarge, we will get to you sometime."

I am thinking, "What a crazy war." "No medical supplies, failing A.C. for our Patients." "God, I hope that our Troops in battle have weapons and ammo."

16 DECEMBER 1967

I get a lead on some medical supplies out at the U.S. Air Force Base, Bien Hoa. My friend, Master Sergeant Greer lets me borrow his five-quarter ton pickup truck for this short trip to the Bien Hoa Air Base. I couldn't believe my eyes, sitting there on the runway is the strangest looking airplane I have ever seen. It has huge very long wings and what looks like bicycle wheels on the wing tips. It is a U.S.A.F. U-2. I was told that there are no U-2's in Vietnam. Oh, Well . . . . Anyway, the U.S. Air Force guys are way laid back and very generous in giving much needed medical supplies.

On the way back to Long Binh I pick up a couple of hitch-hikers. They are U.S. Navy Sea-bees on their way to Long Binh and are grateful for the lift.

I ask, "What do you guys do here in Nam?"

One guy replies, "We are Engineers and our specialty is air-conditioning."

I said, "Man, I sure need someone of your expertise."

One of the guys said, "Sarge, we need some booze for a party and we are not of the pay grade to buy booze."

I say, "How many bottles and what kind?"

Together they said, "Sarge, you no longer have an A.C. problem."

I cannot believe my good fortune. The Sea Bees are good to their word and the A.C. problem is solved. I got them more booze as they needed from time to time and they even gave me several cases of dehydrated shrimp to use for trading material.

20 DECEMBER 1967

The war has got to the point that headquarters put out the word that there is expected to be a large surge in the fighting and that it was possible that an attack from the V.C. and the N.V.A. would come on the Lunar New Year the Vietnamese call TET. The command given out to the 24th Evacuation Hospital is that all Vietnamese patients must be discharged and relocated to Vietnamese medical facilities. All patients to include Baby #2. The entire hospital staff is saddened to think that Baby #2 would be living in the squalid conditions of an orphanage.

That evening, I thought about my options and what I could possibly do to take the baby out of this madness. I went to the Red Cross hut where they have a MARS hook-up where you can call the U.S. if you or your family has a crisis or emergency. The way the system works is that it is a one way connection so at the end of each complete statement you must say "Over" so that the HAM operator can switch the line in the opposite direction. I was able to reach my wife, Else, the first attempt.

I said, "I love you and miss you, Else. Over."

Else replied, "You know I love and miss you very much. Over"

I said, "Listen very carefully, Baby #2 is going to be sent to an orphanage and I have already told you of the orphanage. Over."

Else said, "Rod, what can we do to help. Over."

I said, "I can try to adopt her and care for her until I leave this place. Over."

Else replied, "Yes, do it. We need a baby and the baby needs us. Over."

I said, "I must get off the phone now. I will call you the same time tomorrow and let you give this some serious thought. Be sure you consider everything before you say yes or no. I love you. Over."

After calling my wife I went over to visit the baby. I asked permission from the nurses to take her out for a little while. They let me take her out as it was late evening and not too hot outside. I was able to look at her closely and I can see how beautiful and sweet this little child is. No one knew of my plan to take her home with me, it is a secret I can only share with the baby and my wife for now. The baby seemed to know what I have in mind as she gently touched my face and smiled at me.

THURSDAY

21 DECEMBER 1967

This evening I went over to the Red Cross hut to attempt to call my wife. The Red Cross worker allowed me to make the second MARS call. This call was short and sweet.

I said, "Else, what have you decided? Over."

Else said, "Rod, you bring our baby home and I love you. Over."

I said, "Else, I will do everything possible to bring our baby home. Over."

22 DECEMBER 1967

Today I talk with Captain Devine. I told her of the decision my wife and I had made. I told Virginia I would attempt to adopt Baby #2 and that I knew there would be legal hurdles to solve and overcome, and that I would hire a Vietnamese to look after the baby in my hootch until we could leave Vietnam. Virginia was so excited that she cried.

Virginia said, "I will talk to our Chief Nurse and I will personally see that our baby is taken care of until you leave Vietnam. Also, I will talk to our Hospital Commander, Colonel Leaver, and get his approval."

I said, "What about the Inspectors coming to check for Civilians?"

Virginia said, "Not to worry Sergeant, I will see that our baby is not found."

Captain Devine did talk to the Chief Nurse and The Hospital Commander and all was agreed upon.

The inspectors did come to check and found no civilian patients.

Now my work is cut out for me. First, I asked our Hospital Interpreter to find me a Vietnamese lawyer that can speak English and will take the job I am offering.

26 DECEMBER 1967

Our Hospital Interpreter found a Lawyer gentleman, Mr. Tau.

After our introduction and explaining my plan of adoption to Mr. Tau, he is silent for a while and then Mr. Tau said, "You crazy Sergeant! No one can do this! This impossible!"

I reply, "Thank you for your opinion and comments Mr. Tau, now let's get on with my plan."

First I sent Mr. Tau to the tent city in Saigon to try and find the parents of our baby. Four days later Mr. Tau reported to me that the Tent City is an impossible situation and most of the refugees leave this pathetic place as soon as they can. He explained that there are hundreds of U.S. Army large tents for thousands of people and that the place is filthy, smelly, totally unsanitary and no place for a human to live. He said no one can recall the people we are looking for and the record keeping at tent city is a joke.

Then Mr. Tau said, "Well Sergeant, what your next move?"

I replied, "We will write up documents that will explain that the baby was deserted, and how my wife and I will care for this child with no expense or effort required of the Bien Hoa Province or the Republic of Vietnam."

Mr. Tau said, "This never done before, Sergeant."

I told Mr. Tau, "This will make you famous for being the first, Mr. Tau, now let us make a beautiful presentation and proposal for you to translate and take to the Bien Hoa Provincial Court for consideration."

Mr. Tau said, "You make papers Sergeant, I translate and take to court."

30 December 1967

Having finished my duties for the day, I sit down in my office and began assembling a list of what I thought would be the necessary paper work that might be required of the Bien Hoa Provincial Court. The list included; a Certificate of Birth from the 24th Evacuation Hospital, a statement from our Hospital Interpreter of the mom refusing to take their baby, a brief bio of myself and my wife to include stating our ability to provide and care for the baby, an affidavit from Mr. Tau of his futile search for the baby's family, a statement from my Commanding Officer of my character as being stable as a prospective parent, a letter stating that there will be no future cost or burden for the care of Nguyen Thi Mein to The Bien Hoa Province or The Republic of Vietnam.

Gathering the material for the adoption is a new and challenging experience. I have no knowledge of Law, be it American or Vietnamese. In fact I have never had contact with any Court or Lawyer as I have not even had a traffic ticket or any other violation of the law.

1 JANUARY 1968

New Year's Day did not bring much hope or joy for the New Year as we are still getting too many wounded American Soldiers. Of course, there is always reason for optimism; one reason being that Hanoi did announce in October 1967 that they (the Viet Cong, The National Liberation Front and The North Vietnamese Army) will observe a seven day truce from 27 January through 3 February 1968 for the TET Holiday. This looks to be a possible beginning of the end to this crazy civil war that the U.S.A. has become so deeply involved in. As a matter of fact, The South Vietnamese Military is making public their plans to allow recreational leave for approximately half of its military forces.

2 JANUARY 1968

The Personnel Officer of the 24ᵗʰ Evacuation Hospital notarized & signed the statements and translations for the adoption of Nguyen Thi Mein. We ended up with a decent sized packet of documents for Mr. Tau to take to The Bien Hoa Provincial Court.

5 JANUARY 1968

M r. Tau got back to inform me that The Bien Hoa Provincial Court, after much ridicule and stating they did not want to waste their time processing the adoption request, had accepted the request for the adoption of Nguyen Thi Mein by Leon & Else Rodriguez.

10 January 1968

Baby #2 has her first medical problem. She has a rash on her butt. No surprise, almost everyone has a rash on their butt, groin or armpits. The heat and dust are brutal. The nurses put Baby #2 face down butt up on a small pillow placed in a box on top of a bedside night stand, and had a light shining on her bare butt to dry out the rash. In two days our baby has a clear rash free butt.

15 JANUARY 1968

We are running desperately low on items for doing our never ending Neuro Surgery. We are almost out of cottonoid sponges, Rainy clips (necessary for holding the scalp out of the operating field), silver clips (used for control of bleeding of tiny blood vessels in the brain) and most importantly two of our malleable suction/cautery tips have broken and must be replaced (this instrument is vitally important for the Neuro Surgeon to maintain exposure and cauterize small blood vessels).

The 93rd Evacuation Hospital is about 1 ½ miles from our hospital and I know they do not have a Neuro Surgeon and that they should have the same basic instruments and supplies as our hospital is supposed to have. I take the short Jeep drive over to the 93rd Evacuation Hospital. I was welcomed into the little office of The NCOIC of Surgery and to my most pleasant surprise I had a kind greeting from Sergeant Kemke. Sergeant Kemke and I were stationed together at the 34th General Hospital in Orleans, France from 1956 through 1959. It is wonderful seeing him again.

Kemke says, "I hear you guys at the 24th Evac are busy as hell?"

I reply, "It is because we are the Neuro Surgery & Maxillofacial Center and any patient with just a scratch on his head, regardless of his other injuries, is sent to us."

Kemke says, "Sucks to be you, our causality rate is probably half of what you get."

I ask, "Sergeant Kemke, my friend, we are in desperate need of neuro instruments and neuro supplies. I know that you do not have a Neuro Surgeon, and I know that you should have the same basic neuro instruments and supplies as our hospital, can you help me out?"

Kemke says, "Let's go check it out as to what I can let you have."

In his supply buried away are Rainy clips, bone wax, silver clips, cottonoids. In his instrument room we find malleable suction/cautery tips and Cushing forceps that they have no use for. Thanks to my friend Sergeant Kemke our 24th Evacuation Hospital Neuro Surgeons are still able to save lives.

17 January 1968

Today is my birthday. I am 30 years old. To my men, I am the old man. I certainly don't feel old and I can still keep up with any man, workwise.

Mr. Tau has just come into my office.

I ask, "Mr. Tau, have you heard from the Bien Hoa Provincial Court?"

He replies, "No Sergeant, I don't believe they take your request seriously."

I say, "Mr. Tau, you will re-submit our request for adoption completely as initially prepared and you will add a face sheet with large bold lettering stating that this is the second request for a court hearing. Also, every ten days you will re-submit the same request a third, fourth, fifth time and so on until the court sees our persistence and sincerity for this court action."

Mr. Tau asks, "Sergeant Rodriguez, what is this word 'persistence'?"

I reply, "It means when you do not give up, when you keep trying, do not take 'no' for an answer, when you do what you believe to be right."

Mr. Tau says, "Sergeant, you persistence man."

I said, "Please Mr. Tau, let me know what is happening with our request every ten days."

18 JANUARY 1968

Our inventory of surgical supplies is at the lowest level to date. I am getting into a funk of depression and thinking about how I got myself into this mess of Vietnam. In May of 1967 I was the NCO in charge of Surgeries at the 106th General Hospital at Kishini Barracks in Yokohoma, Japan. Our hospital was formerly an R&R (rest & recuperation) Center left over from the Korean War Era. We converted this place into a 1,000 bed general hospital to care for the injured troops evacuated from Vietnam. I had a perfect job; most of my men were highly skilled technicians that required little if any supervision, other than daily assignments. Our Medical Supply Officer, LTC Dee Bennett, understood our hospital's mission and he always accepted and quickly processed my supply requests, be they standard or non-standard items needed.

My wife, Else, was able to join me in Japan and we had comfortable housing located on a golf course not far from my place of duty. Everything was good. I had this nagging desire to go to Vietnam to be part of the real action. The Commander of The 106th General Hospital, Colonel Charles Reed, was not pleased with my request to go to Vietnam. After the third request I was finally given orders to The Republic of Vietnam. On 17 June 1967 I flew out of Yokota U.S. Air Force Base, Japan on a Braniff Air Lines 707 and landed at the Tan Son Nhut U.S. Air Base in Saigon, Vietnam. As we landed the rain was coming down so hard on the airplane that it felt as though we were inside a snare drum. As soon as I got out of the plane and onto the wheeled stairs the sirens began to blast and there were warnings of incoming rockets. The pilot of the bright yellow Braniff 707 took off immediately with only a couple of us out of the plane. I had no clue that a 707 could take off so quickly. The terminal was a short distance away. I jogged over to the terminal to get out of the soaking rain. The terminal was deserted except for a young U.S Airman that was in charge. He told me to take cover in a bunker at Camp Alfa which is just a short distance from the terminal. The Airman asked if I had changed my green back money for MPCs (military payment certificates). I told him I had not; he said he would do it for me. I pulled out my wallet and the wallet and all contents are totally soaked. I had to carefully peel each bill apart to do the exchange. The Airman gave me a small plastic bag to keep my new multicolored money dry and I heard him murmur 'FNG'. I jogged over to a Quonset hut with a sign Camp Alfa. The hut had a desk manned by a young soldier. The hut is filthy; there are a dozen bunks with thin dirty mattresses.

The Soldier in charge said, "Let me have your orders and go to the bunker until the all clear signal is given."

I said, "I will keep my orders for now."

I went out to the bunker and it was filled with dirty water and trash. I opted to hunker down near a slab of concrete that had a little cover from the rain. Suddenly, the sirens quieted, the rain stopped and there was activity of men, airplanes and trucks. I went back into the Camp Alfa hut and asked the clerk what the routine is for incoming personnel, if any. He told me that most troops coming through Camp Alfa were picked up by their assigned unit, and only a few stayed overnight.

He said I would be picked up tomorrow and transported to the 90th Replacement Depot at Long Binh Army Post. I asked him where Long Binh Army Post is located and he told me about 30 clicks (kilometers) to the north on the Saigon-Bien Hoa Highway. I thanked him and headed for the Tan Son Nhut Air Base main gate. I hitched a ride on a deuce-an-a-half truck filled with armed U.S. Soldiers of the 199th Light Infantry Brigade. The Lieutenant in charge said they were driving right past the 90th Replacement Depot and I was welcome to ride with them. The Soldiers in the back of the truck were laughing at my wet uniform. They are in complete combat attire; weapons, flak jackets, steel pots, jungle fatigues and ponchos. I am wearing a wet summer uniform of T.W.s (tropical worsteds) and a wet green service hat. Again, I heard "FNG" (F—king new guy).

Then one of the troops said, "Hey, this Sergeant is a medic, see the Caduceus on his collar,"

After that they were all friendly, knowing that I might be the medic that saves their ass.

The 90th Replacement Depot is a series of large tents. The sergeant in charge checks my orders and records and said I was up to date with my inoculations, administrative requirements and familiarization with the rifle and pistol. All I needed was a complete issue of combat uniforms and tomorrow I would be sent to my new assignment. I asked what and where I was assigned.

He said, "See those Quonset huts with the large water tank, the heliport and the red cross marker. That is your new home."

I said, "I can walk over there and save you having me around."

He said, "After we issue your uniforms, we will take you there in my jeep, Good Luck."

I found the Detachment Headquarters of the 24th Evacuation Hospital and signed in. I was directed to my hootch. It is the Senior NCO tent. I had a folding cot, mattress, pillow, clean sheets & pillow case and most importantly my cot had mosquito netting.

18 JUNE 1967

After enjoying an excellent breakfast in our hospital mess hall, I wandered over to the surgical huts and introduced myself. They are very busy with two craniotomies, a thoracotomy, various general surgeries and several orthopedic cases going on. Not wanting to be in the way I went back to my hootch. As it was Sunday most of the Senior NCOs were there; 1st Sergeant Ed Zehel, Master Sergeant Greer (Chief Ward Master), Sergeant First Class Smith (Mess Sergeant), Sergeant Johnson (Motor Pool NCO). They welcomed me and gave me helpful information.

19 June 1967

After meeting the Detachment Commander and processing through the Personnel Office I went to my place of duty. Sergeant First Class Valdez is the man I will replace. He was anxious to be relieved and return to his family and the land of the big P.X. I asked SFC Valdez of the duties he was responsible for.

He said, "Making the enlisted men's assignments, ordering supplies and doing maintenance on surgery equipment." Sergeant Valdez showed me around the two huts that housed the Operating Room areas with five Operating Tables in each hut; a third hut housed the Centralized Material Section (CMS), which did the sterilization of supplies and instruments for the entire hospital. Behind the CMS hut is a large tent where the six field autoclaves (sterilizers) run for 24 hours a day, seven days a week. The autoclave job is hot, wet and dangerous. Behind the two surgery huts are two deuce-an-a half trucks, one of the trucks holds the emergency generator which can produce enough electrical power to run all the surgery lights, the air-conditioners and other necessary surgical equipment. I thanked Sergeant Valdez for the information. Sergeant Valdez left country the next day.

The Surgery Staff was surprised when they found that I was participating in every function of surgery in addition to making assignments, ordering supplies and maintaining equipment. I helped with the never ending cleaning of the bloody mess in surgery; also I love to scrub and first assist in all specialties of surgery. I helped the nurses circulate and provide sterile supplies to the scrub technicians.

Except for the constant lack of supplies my job became routine.

I must tell you of my men; these guys are 19 to 26 years old, bright, professional and anxious to learn more about surgery so they can enable the surgeons to do the best job possible for our troops. My outstanding men are Jack Henderson, Bill McGillvary, John McDonald, Andy Pope and Bill White. There are many other good men, but the mentioned are my heroes as they can and will assist on all the major challenges of combat surgery.

The Nurses are all highly competent and devoted to excellent Patient care. Major Mary Jane Carr is the Nurse in Charge of Surgery and CMS. Mary Jane Carr is a beautiful woman. So very petite, maybe five feet tall. This lady always has a smile, 'can do' attitude and is very concerned for all her surgery family. The Surgery Staff loves Mary Jane.

The Staff Nurses I am most impressed with are Sue Olson—A young, pretty, sweet and hard-working Nurse, Jane Gardner—Always smiling, always positive, Josephine Palmari—This Nurse was always psyched up for even the most horrible trauma, Katy Coombs—The consummate professional, Bob Springer—A male Nurse that can and will do it all, from the dirtiest, bloodiest and most challenging surgery. Bob is a good man.

The Anesthesia Staff are incredible. The anesthesia machines (apparatus) are left over from the Korean War Era. There are no ventilators, so when complete paralyzation is required for a specific surgical case, regardless of the time required for the procedure, the anesthesia person must hand ventilate for the patients survival, this is a big deal. The anesthesia equipment and the anesthesia drugs are so primitive and basic it is only because of the high competence and great effort that our patients have excellent anesthesia care.

The Surgeons; Doctors Kern, Beazley, Graff, Averbach, Jelsma, Robinson, Dean, Leaver, Patrick, Gonzales and so many more outstanding Surgeons are committed to giving their best patient care possible to our troops, regardless of their feelings as to our Country's involvement in this crazy Vietnamese civil war.

Our U.S. Servicemen, as severely wounded as some of them are, never cry out, or scream, or carry on. If they talk at all, they ask about their wounded buddy. These Troops are my brave, valiant heroes.

My depression is because I am out of control in not being able to get the medical supplies necessary to do our mission. I feel that I am personally letting down our Patients, our Doctors, our Nurses and our Corpsmen.

19 JANUARY 1968

I t is 2000 hrs. (8 P.M.) I have finished with all I can do for the day. The night shift is in good shape and working smoothly. I decide to find the Long Binh Post Beer Tent and get drunk. I have not had much to drink since I left Japan. Tonight I will try to escape my situation with a bad hangover. I found the large circus shaped beer tent that had saw-horses with plywood on top for a bar, lots of card tables and folding chairs. The music was blasting from reel to reel tape decks with the large loud speakers and the air was clouded with thick blue smoke from the stinky smokers. I found an empty table and set down with a can of beer in each hand.

I heard a loud voice, "Hey Sergeant Rod!"

I looked up and it was Murphy. Murphy was the unit Armorer for the 128th Evacuation Hospital in Ludwigsburg, Germany when I was stationed there in 1960. Murphy was a Corporal back then, but now he is wearing Master Sergeant Stripes. He did an excellent job as unit Armorer; maintaining the unit's weapons and being accountable for the entire Unit's ammunition. Murphy is the kind of guy that just shaved, but looked like he had three day old stubble. Also, Murphy always looks sloppy; his uniform is always baggy and ill-fitting even if he just broke starch.

I said, "Murphy, good to see you. Congratulations to you on your promotions. What are you doing here in Nam?"

Murphy said, "I am the NCOIC of the Medical Depot. We are in process of moving from Cholon to Long Binh. Cholon is in the Chinese section of Saigon. This huge move and building process has taken three months and we have much yet to do."

I said, "Murphy, I am having a hell of a time getting medical supplies and if I don't get some ASAP my hospitals mission will be compromised. Can you help?"

Murphy said, "Your Medical Supply Officer must not have read the message we sent out regarding our move. We told all the unit Medical Supply Officers to over stock and if they needed any item in an emergency we would take care of it."

I said, "Murphy, I need supplies now!"

Murphy said, "Rod, you get me a list of your needs and I will fill it for you."

I said, "You wait right here and I will be back before you can drink these two beers."

I doubled timed it back to my office and picked up the four page requisition list of needed supplies and hustled back to the beer tent and gave the list to Murphy.

Murphy said, "This is a big order, do you have a truck?"

I replied, ""Yes, a deuce-an-a-half."

Murphy said, "I will have your stuff on the loading dock at the Cholon Medical Supply Depot at 1400 hours Sunday, let me draw you a map with directions to Cholon."

Murphy and I had another beer and talked of the good times in Germany. I left Murphy with a firm handshake and a guarantee from Murphy that he will provide the medical supplies.

I cannot sleep Friday or Saturday night, I was filled with excitement and anticipation.

MORNING
20 JANUARY 1968

I am off duty and I ask one of my off duty men if he will go with me to Cholon. He was happy to leave Long Binh and to break his routine for the day. We fueled up the truck, checked the oil and made sure the truck is good for our trip. The drive down the Saigon-Bien Hoa Highway is uneventful. We crossed over the Saigon River on the Newport Bridge. Then the traffic was almost complete chaos. There are oxen pulled carts, mopeds. bicycles, trucks, cars, tanks, jeeps and too many people. Getting through Saigon is slow and difficult, especially getting through the round-abouts. Finally, out of the main part of the city of Saigon on the road adjacent to a golf course (I didn't know there was a golf course in Vietnam) to the west of us. On the 17th hole there are ARVNs chasing Black Pajama clad V.C. and we can hear the steady crack of automatic rifle fire. We did not slow down as I had no desire to be collateral damage. We stayed on the road around the golf course and as we passed the 1st hole there are people lined up to tee off. "What a weird war." Finally we arrived at the Medical Depot in Cholon and true to his word Master Sergeant Murphy is with three of his men on the loading dock with my medical supplies. We quickly and carefully load cases of Ringers, D5W and saline solutions, plaster bandages, sponges, instruments, light bulbs, suture, knife blades, salt tablets, hydrogen peroxide, etc., etc. until my lists are filled. I hugged Sergeant Murphy and promised him a big steak dinner if and when we meet again. On our way back to Long Binh the trip past the golf course was uneventful and going through the round-abouts in Saigon was difficult. When we slowed down the young Vietnamese men would try to jump on our truck in attempting to steal some of our supplies.

Finally we crossed the Newport Bridge on our final leg of our trip to Long Binh. We got home to the 24th Evacuation Hospital and had lots of help unloading our supplies. It was like little kids opening Christmas packages.

Tonight I am thinking back to my training at the 7th U.S. Army NCO Academy at The 10th Special Forces Training compound in Bad Tolz, Germany, where it was drilled into us that being prepared for anything is key to survival and being an NCO you have responsibilities to and for others in accomplishing the unit mission and these responsibilities can make the difference of fellow soldiers living or dying. I slept well this night, thanks to my friend Master Sergeant Murphy.

22 JANUARY 1968

The work-load has slowed, casualties are down and the stress is less. Still no word from the Bien Hoa Provincial Court. Baby #2 looks great and is getting lots of love and attention.

29 JANUARY 1968

I meet with Mr. Tau. Still no word of a court date. Mr. Tau tells me his visits to the court are met with displeasure. I tell Mr. Tau to keep his wonderful smile for them and to take gifts of cigarettes or booze if necessary, but, that he must keep submitting our request every ten days.

Mr. Tau says, "I do for you, Sergeant Persistence."

30 JANUARY 1968
@ 2245 HRS.

All hell breaks loose. The explosions are unbelievable, the noise is terrifying, the earth seems to be floating, the smell of cordite, sulfur & gun powder are strong, the air is filled with smoke, the sky to the immediate north is lit up like a million 4th of July fireworks. I dress quickly and head for surgery. I can hear the sirens giving the in-coming rocket alert and people are screaming, "Go to the bunkers." On my way to surgery an incredible flash lights up the entire sky, as though it is a bright day for a few seconds, then a blast throws me to the ground and a loud noise makes my ears ring. I get off the ground and look up, I can see Huey Helicopter Gunships but I can barely hear the familiar "Whop, Whop, Whop" of their rotor blades, there is a Cobra Helicopter following close behind, and also there is a slow flying fixed wing air craft, which is a AC47-Spooky, commonly called "Puff the Magic Dragon." Then I can hear the unforgettable sound of Gatling Guns. These aircraft are laying down fire around the perimeter of Long Binh Post. The gun-fire looks like a bright orange liquid pouring from a giant watering can, but I know it is tracer-tipped bullets, with every 7th round is a tracer variety on the ammo belt. I continue my run to surgery without incident. The surgery huts are shaking, debris and dust is everywhere. The Doctors, Nurses and Technicians are protecting the Patients with their own bodies. The lights are flickering; the emergency lanterns are all on. Most of the field operating room spot light bulbs have burned out from the fluctuation of the electricity and the Nurses are holding flashlights so the Surgeons can continue to work. Specialist Andy Pope runs outside to the deuce-an-a-half truck with the emergency generator and fires it up. The lights, air-conditioners, suctions and cauteries are again working. I quickly change the burned out spot light bulbs and help where needed. There is no fear or chaos in surgery, everyone just goes to work. The monster explosions abate after about 30 minutes, and then there is the constant sound of major explosions.

What has happened is that two pods of the ammo dump have been ignited. The ammo dump is located less than two miles north of the 24th Evacuation Hospital. Word is that V.C. sappers got into the ammo dump and detonated 15 plus satchels of explosives; also another ammo pod was hit with a freak 122mm rocket. The ammo dump continued to explode for many days and nights.

"Needless to say, The Hanoi truce is a lie."

There were other things more threatening than the ammo dump explosion that we were unaware of. About ten minutes before the ammo dump blew up a party of Australian Officers we're leaving the 93rd Evacuation Hospital Officers Club, when they flew out in their helicopter they spotted hundreds of N.V.A and V.C. Soldiers waiting for the order to invade Long Binh Post. The Aussies reported their find to our U.S. Army Air Defense Command and they immediately sent out a chopper to confirm this situation. Upon seeing the impending attack the Huey Gunships, Cobras and Puff the Magic Dragon were dispatched with Gatling Guns and other fire power. They laid down fire that I could see and it was absolutely incredible, thus saving lives of hundreds of American troops.

There was major chaos, but not in surgery, we all knew what to do and did it. Days and nights for over a week we are overwhelmed with causalities. The triage work done by Captain Caroline Tanaka and her E.R. Doc's saved many lives. Most all civilians wounded were put in ambulances and sent to Vietnamese hospitals. I tried to limit my men to twelve hour shifts, but many would not take relief if they were helping with a crisis surgery. Major Mary Jane Carr worked 36 hours straight without rest.

Major Carr came to me and said, "Sergeant Rod, I cannot keep up with you, I must get some rest, Sue Olson will lead the night shift and Jane Gardner will lead the day shift."

I said, "Major Carr, I have also lost track of time, I will rest soon, but for now I have much to do. Go rest, we will hold down the fort for you."

Words of Doctor Donald Patrick, Surgeon, "Our abilities to function at a fever pitch for days at a time ignoring hunger and sleeplessness while expending our maximum efforts to care for the maimed and dying."

Thank God and Master Sergeant Murphy, I do not have to worry about supplies, all I have to do is look out for my men and help the Surgeons.

TUESDAY

31 JANUARY 1968

T he electricity has been restored and the surgery huts withstood the huge blasts with only minor damage. Since we now have outside electricity I drive the deuce-an-a-half truck with the emergency generator to the P.O.L. (petroleum, oil & lubricants) station for a topping off of fuel for the generator, just in case we lose power again. On the way to the P.O.L. station I see several large trucks pulling outsized flatbed trailers being loaded with bodies of the N.V.A & V.C. that had been killed by our choppers and Puff the Magic Dragon the previous night. There are hundreds of bodies stacked like cordwood. Another astounding sight to me was the tanks and artillery pieces that ringed Long Binh Post. I didn't know there were that many tanks in the world. If anyone had ambitions of invading our post again, they would have a hell of a time doing it.

I take time to check on Baby #2.

Captain Devine says, "I was expecting you to visit. Our Baby is in safe hands with the Nurses, Corpsmen and Patients in the medical ward."

I said, "Thank you Captain, I knew you would handle the situation."

I am relieved to hear this as I know that Captain Devine and her staff are overwhelmed with causalities and post-operative Patients. The Medical Ward is not busy at all as most of their patients are healthy

& ambulatory. The grunts in the field refer to this class of patients as "Profiles." That label is given to this group of Patients that have a medical problem to get out of combat or another dirty job. For the most part, these are actually good guys that have the misfortune (or fortunate) to have a non-communicable disease or problem like bleeding hemorrhoids, anal fistula, cycle cell or some exotic rash. Anyway, these people do take good care of Baby #2 in our time of need.

TET brought us some truly sad situations. An Eye Surgeon came into surgery carrying a toddler with one eye dangling out of its socket. The Surgeon wanted to bring the baby immediately into surgery in hopes of saving the child's eye. All of our operating room tables are occupied and there are many severely wounded American Troops waiting surgery and the hospital policy is to take care of our troops first. We offered instrumentation and recommended he try the E.R. Mary Jane Carr cried at not being able to care for this child and I felt a great heaviness in my chest for being helpless to help this baby.

10 FEBRUARY 1968

The causalities are still overwhelming. A Chinook Helicopter lands with twelve litter cases of seriously injured soldiers and ten walking wounded, all require surgery. Ten minutes later another Chinook Helicopter landed with the same number of wounded soldiers. The Huey air Ambulances and Gunships are landing continuously with four to six wounded troops needing surgery. Captain Tanaka and her crew are busy to the maximum.

Another 24th Evacuation Hospital group that must be praised is the guys of the x-ray & laboratory. They always keep up with great x-rays and blood work. The lab guys always have blood or plasma for transfusions which there is a huge demand.

We are told the U.S. Troops achieved a decisive military victory over the enemy during the TET offensive, but suffered an equally conclusive political and psychological defeat from the U.S. Media, craven Politicians and the U.S. Peace Movements.

TET has been a traditional celebration that brings the Vietnamese a sense of hope, happiness and peace. TET reminds me of death, suffering, bitter memories and tears.

13 FEBRUARY 1968
@ 1500 HRS.

A HU-1 Helicopter Air Ambulance unloads a 1st Cavalry Trooper with a blood soaked O.D. green towel wrapped around his head and he has a field type tracheostomy bleeding slightly at his throat. When he is taken into the E.R. Captain Caroline Tanaka carefully removes the towel from the wounded soldier's head. Even the combat veteran U.S. Army Nurse, Captain Tanaka is shocked at the severity of the injuries. Calmly she checked to insure that this Soldier has a good airway, had been given morphine to ease the pain, checked his vital signs and then sweetly comforts him. His name is Rory Bailey. Rory Bailey had just turned twenty and he had sustained injuries that blew away both of his eyes, his eye sockets, his nose, his upper jaw, his lower jaw and his tongue. Rory has forever lost his speech, his sense of taste, his sense of smell, his vision and cannot speak. Rory has lost his face. Captain Tanaka immediately alerted surgery that we had a top priority case. Captain Tanaka started two large bore I.V.s and sent Rory through the lab & x-ray, then a brief stay in pre-op and then into surgery. The Maxillofacial Surgeons now have the greatest challenge of their careers. One of my best Technicians, 20 year old Jack Henderson, volunteered to assist & scrub with the Maxillofacial Surgeons. Unbelievably with all this head and face trauma there is no C.S.F. (cerebral spinal fluid) leak and no brain damage. Rory was on the operating room table over 18 hours. We offered Jack Henderson, the scrub tech, relief, but this outstanding Technician and Soldier refused to leave Rory and the Surgeons until they had done all possible for this Patient. Rory left the 24th Evacuation Hospital two days later in an air ambulance to the U.S.A.

*Years later Rory Bailey was on the cover of Life and People Magazines as the man with no face. Rory lived to be 60 years old.

16 February 1968
@ 1700 hrs.

I walked over to the E.R. to see if we had a back log of patients other than what is waiting in Pre-op. A dust-off chopper landed and was off-loading a young pregnant Vietnamese lady. The entire back of this young lady's skull was gone and brain tissue was all over her upper torso. She had intermittent labored breathing (Cheyne-Stokes) and she was taken into the E.R. and a Cesarean section was done in hopes of saving the baby. The baby girl is as beautiful as an angel. The baby's lungs are not sufficiently developed to maintain life and she soon dies. I had to quickly walk away as I could not hold back my tears.

The rest of the month of February 1968 was a blur of surgical trauma that was almost overwhelming. The good part is I can now get medical supplies on request.

1 MARCH 1968

Today I meet with Mr. Tau. He always wears a white shirt, black tie, black trousers, black shoes and a friendly smile. Today his smile is larger than usual.

Mr. Tau says, "Sergeant Rodriguez, we have a court date!"

I am so happy that I hug Mr. Tau.

I say, "Mr. Tau, this is wonderful. When is our court date? Do we need more paper-work or additional documents?"

He replies, "The court date is 2:00 P.M. 22 March. No Sergeant, they want no more papers."

I am thinking this could be a good thing or this could be a bad thing.

2 MARCH 1968

I meet with a Green Beret buddy to give him two cases of dehydrated shrimp to take to the orphanage. I can only give him a case or two of shrimp at a time; if I give him more the V.C. will come in and shoot the orphanage up to get the food supplies. This Special Forces friend needs some Foley catheters for their ARVN Medical Unit. He is in luck as I have a good stock and can afford to give up a couple of dozen.

He tells me, "Someone fouled up and ordered Fogarty catheters instead of Foley catheters and they won't work as bladder drains."

This is music to my ears.

I said, "I desperately need Fogarty catheters, may I have them?"

He said. "Absolutely, they are only 3mm to 5mm and could only work possibly on an infant."

I said, "Fogarty's are not intended for bladder drainage. I have dire need for them in reconstructing arteries, thus saving arms, hands, legs and feet of our troops."

He told me to follow him to the ARVN Special Forces Camp near the town of Tam Hiep. Driving through Tan Hiep was hell. There are bloating corpses laying in the gutters. There are large signs that said, "Off Limits to all U.S. Military Personnel. Do Not Stop."

When we got to the ARVN Special Forces Camp I can see their once lovely clean swimming pool is now stained with blood and there are body parts floating around. Obviously there had been one hell of a fight right here. I picked up the Fogarty catheters and quickly drove back to the safety of Long Binh Post.

8 MARCH 1968

Time drags on since Mr. Tau has given me the court date and all the days seem longer.

Today I stick to my usual routine, shower at 0500 hrs., get dressed and go to the mess hall. The mess hall doesn't start to serve until 0600 hrs. But they let me have two slices of toast and a large glass of orange juice. By 0530 hrs. I am in the Operating Room huts doing the never ending maintenance and repair of the suction machines, the cautery apparatus and the surgical spot lights. The suction machines frequently overflow from the copious amounts of irrigation fluids and the large amount of blood from wounds. The suctions are an easy repair as I do it almost daily. The cautery apparatus are antiques left over from the Korean War Era and are very primitive and dangerous. The main repair I do on the cautery machine is to reset the spark gap. Inadvertently the knob for the spark gap gets turned during prolonged surgeries or during cleaning the machine. The spark gap must be set correctly or the patient could suffer burned tissue with too much power or on the other hand there would not be sufficient energy to cauterize. All the Surgeons know of this potential so they test the cautery on subcutaneous (fat) tissue before they touch the cautery to brain, bowel or any other sensitive tissue. The surgical spot lights have a constant problem of drifting after a few hours of use. The spot lights are also an easy fix as I just have to tighten and counter-tighten the bushings on the swivel arm.

After my maintenance chores I visit Baby #2. Our baby is sound asleep in spite of the constant flurry of activity and noise around her.

I go back to the operating room huts and see that the Maxillofacial Surgeons are finishing up a facial reconstruction on a young soldier that took an AK-47 round to his face. They have done a magnificent job plating the left orbit (eye socket), wired his broken jaw and are now doing a beautiful plastic skin closure. On the adjacent O.R. table Nurse Sue Olson is very carefully prepping the blackened skin of a soldier whose body is 70% burned by napalm. I can see the tears in Sue Olson's eyes as she gently preps the burns and watches large pieces of skin tissue flake off leaving a reddened sub-dermal tissue. Napalm sticks to the skin and burns it black. Napalm is gelled petroleum with naphthenic acid. After the surgeons treat the burn patients other injuries his burns are slathered with ointment and carefully dressed and bandaged. As soon as this patient wakes up from his anesthetic he will be immediately shipped out to a cleaner environment for further treatment (Japan or the U.S.A.). As usual, there are two craniotomies going on with the surgeons, nurses, techs and anesthesia completely consumed with the task at hand. There are two O.R. tables with Ortho Docs fixing multiple fractures. There is another O.R. table with a Vascular Surgeon applying a long leg cast on a Soldier that had his tibial artery severed and put back together by the Vascular Surgeon. The Surgeon is applying the cast so his arterial repair will not be torn apart. The Vascular Surgeon is smiling and pleased to see that his Patient's foot and toes are a bright pink and have excellent pedal pulse. He makes a window in the cast at the ankle area and marks a spot with a marking pen so the nurses can easily find the pulse. This troop just had his lower leg saved. The rest of the O.R. tables have patients with MFWs (multiple fragment wounds), small wounds from shrapnel sprinkled over their entire bodies. These wounds are generally caused by Claymore mines.

In the afternoon there are the usual causalities of war, but there are two that got to me. The first is a young ROK (Republic of Korea) Soldier that had eyes, nose and hands blown off by a booby trap. The Maxillofacial Surgeon's did their best but the guy has a very poor prognosis, plus the Orthopedic Surgeon had to amputate both of the ROK Soldier's hands at the wrist. The second case is a soldier that has been hit with Willie Peter (white phosphorus). The white phosphorus burns deeply into any tissue it touches. The only way to stop white phosphorus is to take away its oxygen. 5% copper sulfate solution assists in neutralization of white phosphorus. The O.R. Staff must take special precautions to prevent being burned themselves while treating this Patient. This poor Soldier has a great deal of suffering ahead of him.

Again, I feel that I must praise the entire Operating Room Staff of Surgeons, Nurses, Technicians and Anesthesia Folks of the 24th Evacuation Hospital. These fine professionals are the exemplification of "Integrity." Being a blue collar type of guy, I define "Integrity" as the "Give a Shit Factor." I know Webster's defines integrity as; high values and principles, actions that produce a good outcome, but I prefer "The Give a Shit Factor."

The Neuro Surgeon is preparing this Soldier for a craniotomy to relieve a sub-dural hematoma

This Soldier was up talking, eating, and ambulating two days later.

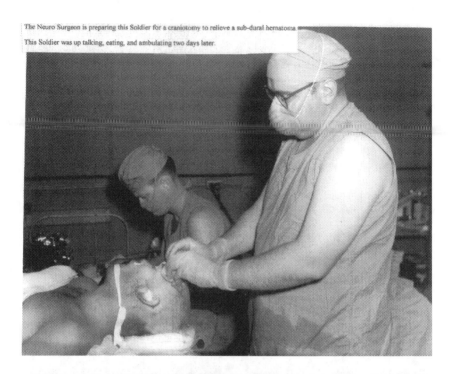

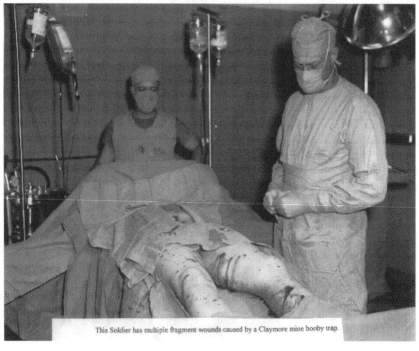

This Soldier has multiple fragment wounds caused by a Claymore mine booby trap.

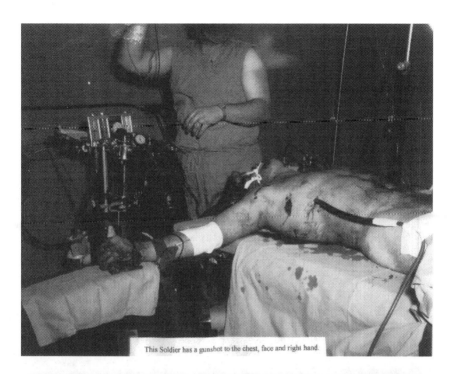

This Soldier has a gunshot to the chest, face and right hand.

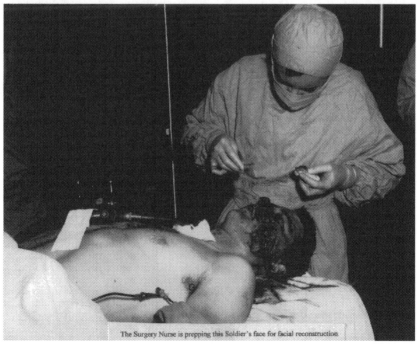

The Surgery Nurse is prepping this Soldier's face for facial reconstruction.

22 March 1968

Finally, the day to go to court has arrived. I do my usual maintenance chores and other duties and get permission to take off after lunch reliefs. I had made arrangements to meet Mr. Tau at 1300 hrs. I am anxious, nervous and excited. The Nurses in ICU/Pre-op/Post-op are all excited as I am. They have Baby #2 dressed in a beautiful pink outfit with pink booties and a pink hat. The Nurses have packed a bag with diapers, ointment for her butt, a bottle of Similac, a baby toy, a light blanket, a damp cloth and extra plastic bags in case the baby peed or pooped. I am instructed to remember that if she voided or pooped I must wipe her from front to back as she is a little girl. Mr. Tau, the baby and I take off for court in an open Jeep. It is an extremely hot and dusty journey.

When we arrived at the Court House Mr. Tau said, "Wait for me here Sergeant, I will get us seats."

Mr. Tau came back and led us through the crowd to our seats. The Court House is a large building with all the windows open and one fan doing a poor job of circulating the air. The building is surrounded with armed ARVN Guards, even inside are armed Guards. The room is hot, humid and stinks. The worst part is the smell of Galois French cigarettes mixed with the smell of Nuoc Mam (fish sauce) and dirty bodies. The crowd watches us and without a doubt we are the new focal point of attention. The room is crowded with people waiting to plead their case. Very few of these people have Lawyers. You can easily recognize the Lawyers as they are dressed just like Mr. Tau, white shirt, black tie, black trousers and black shoes. There are at least 100 people waiting for the judges. There are three Judges sitting elevated behind a large podium. I have never been to a court before and this is not what I expected. It appeared to me that the Judges listens to a person's pleas or statement then issued out a favorable decision or punishment. In each case the Judges heard there is much emotion, screaming, crying and general chaos.

The crowd watches us constantly. I removed our baby's hat and booties to help cool her. Baby #2 is well behaved for the first hour and a half of waiting, and then she wet her diaper. I made a spot on the bench we are sitting on and change her. Every person in the room is straining to see what I am doing. I gather our stuff together placing things back into the bag. Then the baby wants to eat. I find her bottle and gave her half of it, and then I burped her. Baby #2 gives up a loud attention getting belch and everyone, including the guards laugh. The three Judges give me a mean look of distain. Now I began to worry, have I pissed off the Judges? I gave the baby the rest of the bottle and again she gave up a loud burp with the same resulting laughter from the crowd and the Guards. This time the Head Judge banged his gavel and told Mr. Tau that we must be silent and respectful to his court. Now I am seriously concerned. The baby is now smiling and starts to blow bubbles. Suddenly, everyone in the court room began to murmur, smile and point at Baby #2. Even the Judges stood up so they can better see my baby and they also smiled. Then the Head Judge banged his gavel and tells Mr. Tau for us to be quiet.

I whispered to Mr. Tau, "Why are these people smiling and pointing at our baby?"

Mr. Tau says, "Baby blow bubbles."

I said, "All babies blow bubbles."

Mr. Tau says, "In Vietnam when baby blow bubbles mean rain come soon."

I say, "You're kidding me."

Mr. Tau reply, "No, No Sergeant. Rain come when baby blow bubbles."

Finally they motion to Mr. Tau for us to approach the Judge's podium. They have all the paperwork we submitted to include the many duplicate requests. The Head Judge talks with Mr. Tau. Mr. Tau smiles nervously and talks rapidly. Then the judge banged his gavel loudly as he and Mr. Tau have a heated exchange of words. Then I watch a flurry of forms being stamped, waxed and the Judges signing papers.

I asked Mr. Tau, "What is going on?

Mr. Tau replied, "Sergeant, you now have baby to take home."

I am dizzy with joy. This is a major event in my life.

The trip back to Long Binh is a blur. I returned the Jeep to the motor pool, said my goodbyes and thank you to Mr. Tau. I took my baby back to her temporary home in the ICU/Pre-op/Post-op ward. I told the Nurses of our successful adoption hearing and their reaction is pure joy. There is much hugging and everyone smiling. Within a few minutes everyone at the 24ᵗʰ Evacuation Hospital knows the baby has been adopted by Sergeant Rodriguez.

After supper reliefs I go over to the Red Cross hut to call my wife.

I said to my wife, "Hello Else, this is your husband. Over."

Else replied, "It is wonderful to hear your voice, how are you? Over."

I said, "I could not be better! I have good news for you! We are now officially parents! Over."

Else reply, "That is wonderful news. What are the next steps? Over."

I reply, "I must go to the Personnel Office and declare her as my dependent and make arrangements for transportation, but the big deal is getting a visa and passport from the U.S. Embassy in Saigon. Over."

Else says, "According to the news reports Saigon is very dangerous, can you go there? Over."

I say, "I will do whatever it takes. Please do not worry. Over."

Else asks, "Are we going to name our baby Barbara Lynn Rodriguez? Over."

I reply, "If you agree our baby girl is Barbara Lynn Rodriguez. Over."

Else says, "It is a fine name for our baby and I love you both. Over.

I say, "Goodbye for now, I love you and I will tell you more on tonight's audio cassette. Over."

I walked over to the ICU/Pre-op/Post-op and announce that Baby #2 is to be known as Barbara Lynn Rodriguez. The nurses call her Baby Barbara.

25 March 1968

After lunch reliefs I walk over to the 24th Evacuation Hospital Personnel Office. I talk with Lieutenant Dunlevy, the officer in charge, and he assisted in logging in of my new dependent, Barbara Lynn Rodriguez aka Nguyen Thi Mein. Lt Dunlevy and I discuss what I ask of the U.S. Embassy to get a visa and passport.

29 MARCH 1968

I began my journey to the American Embassy in Saigon. The road from Long Binh to the Newport Bridge is uneventful. Along the Saigon-Bien Hoa Highway are vendors selling large green melons, flip flops made from old discarded tires, conical straw hats and gasoline & diesel fuel in 5 gallon U.S. metal containers. The shacks along the highway are built from discarded U.S. wooden shipping pallets. The walls and roofs are made from empty Coca-Cola, Budweiser, Carling Black Label and Schlitz aluminum cans that have been flattened out and serve as shingles. After crossing the Saigon River on the Newport Bridge and getting into Metro Saigon there is massive destruction everywhere, bombed out buildings are still smoldering and smoking. Jeeps, oxen carts, bicycles, cars, tin roofs, bricks and mortar are all mixed together in shambles.

There are many children and their mothers in pathetic condition begging in the streets. There are sounds of occasional rifle fire. Also the comforting sounds of 105mm & 155mm U.S. Artillery explosions nearby. I say comforting sounds as I know that the potential enemy is busy running for cover and not interested in me. I find my way to the American Embassy and the U.S. Marine Guard checks my I.D. and lets me into the Embassy compound. The clerk at the information desk tells me I must get an appointment with the American Embassy Vice-Consul and that can be done by his Secretary, Miss Turtle. I find the Vice-Consul's office and Miss Turtle. I try to explain to Miss Turtle my needs for a visa and passport for my daughter.

Miss Turtle said, "Sergeant, can't you see that there is a war outside and you want to take one these people to America?"

Keeping my cool as there is much on the line, I loudly said to Miss Turtle, "This is a six month old baby girl that has not yet learned to hate and does not know of war, besides this is not your business, just get me an appointment with the Vice-Consul!!"

At that moment the Vice-Consul, Mr. Thompson, came out of his office.

He said. "Sergeant, I've heard about you and the baby girl at the 24th Evacuation Hospital. Have you got time to talk now?"

I excitedly replied, "Yes Sir now is a perfect time."

We went into his large well-appointed office. In front of his desk are three leather covered chairs. Also, in this large room is a huge conference table with a dozen chairs around it. Behind his desk hung an American Flag and the U.S. Embassy Seal. We sat down and I told him our baby's story and my need of a passport and visa. Mr. Thompson listened patiently and was taking notes.

When I finished he said, "Sergeant, you have made my day. I will do whatever it takes to get the passport and visa. Here is a list of documents and paperwork we will need completed so we can start action. Get them to me as soon as possible. Will you need an escort to get out of Saigon?"

I said, "No Sir, I will be back to you soon. Thank you Sir."

Traveling back through Saigon was uneventful and as usual I felt safer after crossing the Newport Bridge onto the open Saigon-Bien Hoa Highway headed for Long Binh.

1 APRIL 1968

I began assembling the necessary paper-work: translations and originals of adoption, proof that Nguyen Thi Mein is my legal dependent and a declaration from my Commanding Officer that all documents are fact and then I must get three photos of my daughter for the passport.

9 APRIL 1968

After lunch reliefs I drive to Saigon with a packet filled with all the required forms, certificates and passport photos. The 33 kilometer trip south down the Saigon-Bien Hoa Highway is easy until getting into Metro Saigon where the traffic is either crawling or stopped. At a round-about I am behind a small convoy of U.S. Marines.

We are stopped for twenty minutes when I got out of my jeep and went to the Marine lead vehicle and asked the Marine Lieutenant, "What is the holdup Lieutenant?"

He said, "There was a firefight just ahead of us and things are being swept up."

He looked at me in a strange way and said, "What the hell are you doing here Gunny?"

I reply, "I have some important papers to deliver to the American Embassy."

I guess I did look out of place without a weapon, steel pot or flak jacket.

The Lieutenant said, "That is where we are going, get your Jeep behind mine and keep up, we'll get you there."

I saluted him and said, "Yes Sir, Thank you Sir."

After getting into the Embassy compound I went directly to the Vice-Consul's office. I was met by Miss Turtle.

She said, "Sergeant, don't you know that we have been under fire today. We really do not have time for you."

I said, "Let Mr. Thompson know that I am here."

Reluctantly she buzzed his office and I heard him say for me to wait for ten minutes. I thanked Miss Turtle.

In less than ten minutes Mr. Thompson came out and greeted me warmly. He checked over the papers.

He said, "This will do the job, Sergeant, I will call the number at your personnel office that you gave me as soon as we have your visa and passport."

I thanked him and began my exciting return trip to Long Binh. I got out of Saigon without incident. To my surprise the four lane Newport Bridge had two lanes blown out by V.C. sappers. They had blown two lanes out of the middle of the bridge on the east side. Traffic was cut to single lanes of vehicles going north and south. The U.S. Army Corps of Engineers said the bridge was stable enough for light wheeled traffic. The Newport Bridge looked like a giant creature had bitten out a large middle section. The rest of the trip to Long Binh was easy.

This scene is one week after The TET Offensive in Saigon.

Scenes of war along the roadside on one of my many trips to The American Embassy in Saigon.

9 MAY 1968

M ajor Mary Jane Carr, The Head O.R. Nurse, came into my office and said, "Sergeant Rodriguez, we have an injured Soldier that is believed to have an unexploded device in his abdomen. This has the potential of killing or injuring our Staff Members that help in attempt to remove it."

Major Carr Asked, "Who will you assign to scrub and assist the Surgeons?"

I replied, "I will scrub and assist the Surgeons. Who will you assign to be the circulating nurse?"

Major Carr Said, "I will be the Nurse."

I said, "Let's go do it."

The Soldier has a large metal object torn into his abdomen that appears on x-ray to be a standard Soviet RGD-5 hand grenade. These grenades can be launched by an AK-47 Rifle. After all precautions had been made to protect the rest of the O.R. Staff the patient was brought into the O.R. The Surgeon cautioned the Anesthesia Person that there could be no coughing, bucking or movement by the Patient. The anesthesia was as smooth as it could possibly be, the endotracheal tube is in place and the Patient is completely paralyzed.

The Anesthesia Provider said, "You are good to go, he's all yours."

Major Carr gently painted the Patient's abdomen with a povodone-iodine solution, and then we draped the Patient. The Surgeon made a three inch connecting incision proximal (above) to the wound and a similar incision distal (below). The muscles and fascia tissues are incised and the peritoneum was enlarged using Metzenbaum scissors. We gently placed large Richardson retractors to provide exposure for the surgeon as he carefully lifted out the metal object and placed the object into a lead-lined container provided by the E.O.D. (explosive ordinance disposal) technician, who then quickly left the O.R. Then we began our usual exploratory laparotomy. We found a tear in the gut and a bruised scraped mesentery (the mesentery is called the policeman of the abdomen and it did its job). A short bowel resection was done and anastomosed with an inner layer of swedged on 3-0 chromic and the outer layer was sutured with interrupted 4-0 silk. The small bleeders on the mesentery were tied off with 3-0 plain suture. A thorough irrigation was done and an inspection was made to insure there are no other injuries.

All visible arteries are pulsing, the ureters are smoothly peristaltic, and the liver, spleen and kidneys look fine. The Surgeon does one final irrigation, places distal and proximal 7/8" Penrose drains and closed up. The Patient is moved onto Post-op awake and in excellent condition.

The E.O.D. technician said that this was not an explosive device.

31 MAY 1968

The Hospital Personnel Officer calls me into his office.

Lt. Dunlevy says, "Sergeant Rodriguez, I have been notified by the American Embassy that all paper work is complete and you can pick up your daughter's passport and visa."

I am pleased beyond belief. Everything is coming together. I run over to ICU/Pre-op/Post-op hut and hold my baby and tell Captain Devine that we are good to go. Everyone is happy and excited.

FRIDAY

7 June 1968

I head out again in an open Jeep south to travel the 33 kilometers to the American Embassy in Saigon. I do not care what obstacles I might encounter. My sole mission is to get to the Embassy. There are the usual slowdowns, but nothing to cause alarm. After arriving inside the Embassy compound I went directly to the Vice-Consul's Office. Of course, Miss Turtle is in a panic and told me Mr. Thompson is very busy and that I must come back another time. I walked past her desk and opened the Vice-Consul's door. He was indeed very busy with more Stars and Eagles (General Officers & Colonels) than I had ever seen gathered together in one room.

I meekly said, "Excuse me gentlemen, I will wait outside."

Mr. Thompson stood up and said, "Sergeant Rodriguez, I've been expecting you. Your choice, you may wait here or wait outside with Miss Turtle."

I said, "Thank you Mr. Thompson, I will wait outside with Miss Turtle."

Five minutes later the conference is over and the Stars and Eagles shuffled out of the office.

Mr. Thompson was all smiles and he said, "Sergeant we did it! Your daughter has a passport and visa. You can take her home."

All I can say is a simple thank you as words cannot express my gratitude, joy and happiness.

Mr. Thompson said, "Here is my personal card, if I can ever help you again, please let me know."

The Vice-Consul, Mr. Thompson, hugged me and firmly shook my hand and asked me, "Can you get back to Long Binh O.K.?"

I reply, "Nothing can stop me now Sir."

7 JUNE 1968
@ 1930 HRS.

I was back in the Red Cross hut making a MARS call to my wife.

"Hello Else, I have good news. Over."

Else says, "Hello Rod. What is it? Over"

I say, "Everything is perfect. I have Barbara's passport and visa in my hand. Over."

Else says, "That is wonderful, I have been so worried. Over."

I say, "Worry no more; we will be home very soon. Over."

Else says, "I love you Over."

I say, "I love you more. I will send an audio cassette tonight and tell you all. Over."

18 JUNE 1968

My replacement is on board and I show him around our surgical complex, and he is anxious to get busy.

This is my last night in Long Binh. The Senior NCOs invite me over to our hospital Enlisted Men's Beer Tent for a farewell toast. The beer tent is divided with 2/3rds for the lower enlisted grades and 1/3 for the NCOs. We have a slab of plywood on saw horses for a bar and ice chests with soda pop and beer. There are a couple of card tables and folding chairs. Pretty fancy bar. One hour into our party, we could hear a fight in the enlisted side of the tent. A canvas fly separates the two areas. I went to see what is happening. There were several Trustees from L.B.J. (Long Binh Jail) beating on a couple of my men. Long Binh Jail (LBJ) is an U.S. Army Stockade that houses the scum of the earth. Mainly they are; murderers, rapists, drug dealers, AWOLs, deserters, fraggers and other bad, bad boys. The lesser criminals (Trustees) are assigned to the shit burning detail. There is no sewer system at Long Binh Army Post so fifty-five gallon oil drums are cut in half and placed in the latrines to catch excrement and toilet paper. This is a hot nasty job with 100 plus degree heat and ninety plus humidity. The job is to pull out the shit filled drums, pour on diesel fuel and ignite. Having been angered at these idiots hurting my men, I jumped in and cold cocked a couple of bullies and the rest of the bums ran away.

My guys said, "Thanks Sergeant Rod, we knew you to be tough, sure glad we didn't rile you."

Actually it felt goooood, kicking some ass. I just imagined it was my nemesis, the clown Medical Supply Officer.

19 June 1968

The Nurses had Baby Barbara bathed and fed. They had a bag containing all necessities for our trip home. I had a small AWOL bag with my basic shaving kit and our paper work. We are ready to catch our jet plane.

The Chief Nurse arranged for us to use the Hospital Commander's air-conditioned sedan for the trip to Tan Son Nhut Air Base. The Chief Nurse, Captain Devine, Baby Barbara and I drove to the airport.

Another round of sweet goodbyes. Barbara got on an Embassy flight, for some reason we could not fly out on a regular commercial Troop flight. We had one single seat for the two of us. I don't care what we fly on; just get me and Barbara home. It turned out the Embassy flight stopped at almost every island in the Pacific. By the time we got to Honolulu I was tired and could use a cold beer. They let us off the plane to go through U.S. Customs; I had a slight panic attack. What if something in our papers or passport is not right? What would I do? The U.S. Customs line moved quickly and we were hustled along; just showing Barbara's passport which they quickly stamped and we were O.K. and in The United States of America without any problem.

I found a bathroom where I could bath and change Barbara into fresh clothes. Our plane was re-fueled and ready to take off, my cold beer can wait. Many hours later we land at Travis Air Force Base, and I get a taxi to San Francisco and board a commercial flight to Denver, Colorado. Then after a short delay we flew to Grand Junction, Colorado. When we got off the DC-3 my wife, Else, was waiting at the bottom of the steps. Else's cheeks are glowing red, her eyes are bright and shining through the tears of joy and her arms outstretched and waiting to hold her new baby and old husband. My Heart is filled with joy with the union of our family. We brought our baby home.

Epilogue

As of this writing my daughter, Barbara Lynn Rodriguez Nipper, is a beautiful, compassionate, sensitive young lady that is forty-four years old. Barbara has been married for over twenty-five years to John Nipper and they have two wonderful children, Josh and Kira. On 10 January 1969 Barbara was baptized into the Catholic Church in the U.S. Army Chapel at Fitzsimons Army Hospital, Denver, Colorado with Captain Virginia Devine and Colonel Robert Leaver being her God parents. Barbara was adopted according to U.S. Law by Else and I the 28th of January 1970. Barbara got her U.S. Citizenship 11 July 1975.

All the wonderful Doctors, Nurses and Corpsmen will never forget the experience of their duties at the 24th Evacuation Hospital during the time period of June 1967 thru June 1968. Most of us still have dreams (nightmares) of the horrors of the Vietnam War, but we are proud of the efforts we made caring for our troops.

I cannot recall any American Serviceman dying in our Operating Rooms. We did lose many Vietnamese Patients, but they arrived into our surgery long after they had been wounded. Doctor Baldwin, one of our Cardio-thoracic Surgeons, attributes our surgical successes to what he calls the "Golden Hour", which means that the injured American Servicemen had an excellent chance of survival if we could get them into surgery within one hour of being wounded.

Most of the Surgeons, Nurses and Corpsmen after leaving the military service became successful in their chosen endeavor. Bill McGillivary, the Corpsman that found the babies to be alive, became an outstanding Physician. Jack Henderson, the Corpsman that worked so hard to help save the soldier with no face became an excellent author of several books and is a successful business man.

AUTHOR
LEON RODRIGUEZ

Born 17 January 1938 in Mesa County, Colorado

Graduated High School June 1955

Enlisted in The U.S. Army in August 1955 at age of 17. Military service overseas; France, Germany, Japan & Vietnam (Vietnam service, June 1967 thru June 1968 & September 1969 thru September 1970). Retired after 20 years of service August 1975. Was awarded numerous awards and decorations to include: The Soldiers Medal (Valor), Two Awards of The Bronze Star Medal, two awards of The Meritorious Service Medal.

Licensed as a Physician's Assistant/Surgical Assistant September 1975 in The State of Washington. Worked as a First Assistant to Surgeons for 32 years. Retired from work July 2007.

Most important and best day of my life was 25 October 1963 when I married Else Heidimarie Muller in Ludwigsburg, Germany.

Other important dates: adoption of my daughter Barbara and son David, and the natural births of my daughters Patricia, Lisa and my son Nick.

My greatest joy is spending time with my kids and grandkids.

"Everyone loves me and I love everyone"

"This guy is asking me to be his kid."

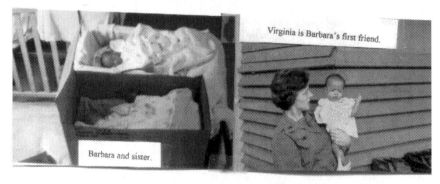

Barbara and sister.

Virginia is Barbara's first friend.

Tanya Moore, Barbara & sister, Patricia

Barbara is 16 years old.

Barbara's Room

VIỆT-NAM CỘNG-HÒA
REPUBLIC OF VIET-NAM
RÉPUBLIQUE DU VIET-NAM

THÔNG-HÀNH
PASSPORT
PASSEPORT

RÉPUBLIQUE DU VIET-NAM

SỔ THÔNG-HÀNH
PASSPORT
PASSEPORT

Số
N°   003242/68

ên, họ
ame   NGUYỄN THỊ MIỄN.
om et prénoms

uốc-tịch
ationality   Vietnamienne
ationalité

igày và nơi sanh
ote and place of birth   26.9.1967 à Biên-Hòa
ieu et date de naissance

ghề-nghiệp
ccupation
rofession

ư-trú
ermanent residence   Long Bình Post, APO
omicile   96491 BIÊN-HÒA

ẫy thông hành này gồm có 44 trang không kể trang bìa
This passport contains 44 pages without the cover.
Ce passeport contient 44 pages non compris la couverture.

— 1 —

HÌNH - DẠNG

Bề cao, Height, Taille .... 0 m 59
Tóc, Hair, Cheveux .... *noirs*
Chân mày, Eye-brow, Sourcils .... *châtains*
Trán, Forehead, Front .... *grand*
Con mắt, Eyes, Yeux .... *noirs*
Mũi, Nose, Nez .... *reliligne*
Miệng, Mouth, Bouche .... *moyenne*
Râu, Beard, Barbe ....
Cằm, Chin, Menton .... *pointu*
Mặt, Face, Visage .... *large*
Dấu riêng, Pecaliarities,
        Signes particuliers |

Có   đứa trẻ cùng đi, tên là :
Accompanied by   children :
Accompagné de   enfants nommés :

Tên, họ Name Nom et prénoms	Ngày sanh Date of birth Date de naissance

Ảnh của đương-sự và, nếu có, của mấy người con
dưới 15 tuổi đi theo.

*Photograph of bearer and children under fifteen who
accompany him (or her).*

*Photographie du titulaire et le cas échéant, des enfants au-
dessous de 15 ans qui l'accompagnent.*

Chữ ký của đương-sự :

Signature of bearer
Signature du titulaire

Sổ thông-hành này có giá-trị để lưu-thông trong
các xứ sau đây:

This passport is valid for the following countries :
Ce passeport est valable pour les pays suivants :

Etats-Unis

Thiếu-Tá TỪ-DƯƠNG

HIỆU-LỰC
VALIDITY — VALIDITÉ

Sổ thông-hành này có hiệu lực đến ngày
trừ khi nào được gia-hạn.   21 Mai
                                  1970
This passport expires on
unless renewed.

Ce passeport expire le
sauf renouvellement.

Cấp tại   Saigon ngày 22 Mai
Issued at   on
Délivré à   le   1968

Thiếu-Tá TỪ-DƯƠNG

GIA - HẠN
EXTENSION OF VALIDITY
PROLONGATION DE VALIDITÉ

Từ ngày | đến |
From | until |
Du | au |

Gia-hạn tại | ngày |
Renewed at | on |
Fait à | le |

— 4 —   — 5 —

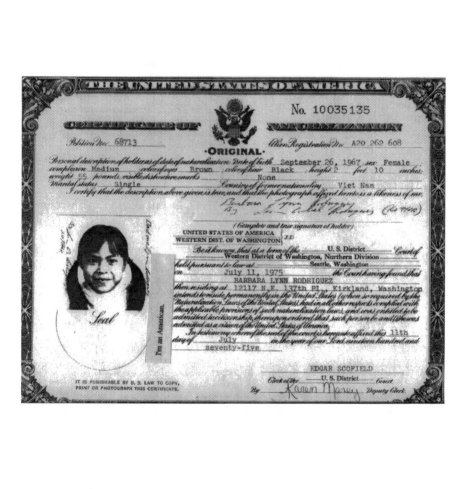

Barbara is 15 years old.

Barbara is 16 years old with sister's Patricia & Lisa and twin brother Nick.